SAVE MONEY GET RICH

A BILLIONAIRE'S TIPS

BRIAN WILLIAMS

Save Money Get Rich

COPYRIGHT@ Brian Williams

Brian Williams

FOREWORD

This book is based entirely on concrete facts with respect to the financial world and experience of successful men in it. No part of this work may be considered fiction or fabrication. All information contained herein is accurate and well-proven facts of the financial aspect of life.

Brian Williams

ACKNOWLEDGEMENT

A special thanks to Ben Simons and other successful businessmen who took the time and trouble to organize interviews and seminars that educated and enlightened so many. It is from this priceless knowledge they impacted on me and my personal experience as a self-made millionaire that the contents of this book were drawn.

Brian Williams

TABLE OF CONTENT

5

Brian Williams

WEALTH PLANNING

Wealth planning, by ordinary definition, is a simple and practical way in which one can manage his or her financial affairs or available assets in order to become wealthy or increase already existing wealth and assets.

Not very many people know this, but wealth planning is responsible for the creation of some of the richest people on earth. A little research shows that a large percentage of these super-rich individuals actually started out poor or with little or no capital for their business, but quickly taught themselves the art of saving money cleverly to become rich. They were so successful in this 'money saving project' that they eventually became world ranking billionaires.

A little more research will show that some of these people, though presently super-rich, still find it difficult to deviate from their successful **money-saving strategies.** These are the same strategies I copied to create mine, which made me wealthy in my own right.

I'm not a billionaire by a long shot and my wealth is nowhere near record-breaking standards, but I presently count my assets in the millions of dollars today because of

7

Brian Williams

my personal wealth management scheme, the basis of which I have put together in this book for you to read.

I learned from the teachings and words of financial tycoons; multi-millionaires and famous billionaires and so can you.

Brian Williams

ITS ALL ABOUT SAVING FROM WHAT YOU'VE GOT

There is a very old English saying that goes, "penny wise, pound foolish". In truth, this saying is a direct reference to shrewd wealth planning. It simply means that even those who have a lot of money but fail to utilize that financial power well enough will lose whatever they have.

On the other hand, those that have little or earn little, but are wise and determined enough to save consistently, even from that little, will be surprised at what they've got saved up at the end of a particular period such as a single year.

Harry, 31, has a salary of just $10,000 a month, but manages to save $3000 out of that each time. At the end of two years, Harry is surprised to find that he has saved more money than he earns in several months. So how much does he have saved up exactly? He has a total of $72,000!

9

Like we pointed out in the beginning, it's all about saving from what you've got. That little you make is what you save from to get better financially.

YOU DON'T NEED A WEALTH PLANNING EXPERT

While there are many professional wealth planning advisers willing to attend to you for a fee, some of the best advice you will ever get on the subject are from real people who have actually managed the little assets they have to become rich. When some of these people share their real-life experience in wealth planning seminars, so many people find it a lot easier to understand and relate.

Once, I came across the sad story of a nice lady in her late 40s who broke down in tears after hearing the speech of a low-level banker who became a self-made millionaire through a simple but clever wealth planning scheme of his own.

When question by the sneaker on what was wrong with her, the story she gave was a simple but a very common one, she has worked for 29 years with nothing to show for it. The speech which was being given by the banker actually made her see the light and it hit home to her heart.

In this book, composed from the priceless knowledge and experience of very wealthy men who got

11

Brian Williams

rich by adequate wealth planning schemes, you get to learn very simple ways to save up the little money you've got and create adequate protection around it.

AVOID THAT DUMB EXCUSE

In today's society where wistfulness is the order of the day, saving money for the future has a negative cliché about it. People give excuses like "I'll rather invest than save" or "Things are so expensive, I never have anything left to save".

What people fail to understand in this circumstance is that the **best investors are actually the best savers and the worst investors are the highest spenders**. If you do not understand what I'm saying, why do you think countries have foreign reserves?

Brian Williams

THE BEST WEALTH PLANNING
STRATEGIES

The best wealth planning strategies are those executed while a person is in his or her prime. Why? The unique subject of wealth planning to grow rich is something that can only be accomplished over a long period of time. Some of the richest people in the world claim that they learned this the hard way and an analysis of their wealth planning schemas prove this to be true.

In the following chapters, we take a closer look at the different wealth planning schemes that answer the question of how to save money to get rich.

Brian Williams

1. Realize The Need to Grow Rich By Saving Money

If you are one of those who believes that no one can ever grow rich in this present age and time by just saving from the little money they've got then you haven't heard about the savings king, billionaire Warren Buffet.

*Who is Warren Buffett?

Warren Buffett, CEO of Berkshire Hathaway is one of the richest men in the world and most of that money comes from saving. This is one man who is considered a "Savings Billionaire" and it reflects in every aspect of his life. He saves so much that his daughter Susie thinks it's embarrassing. He drives a car that is extremely cheap and about a decade out of date, spends less than $3.17 on breakfast, and also lives in an old house he bought for just $31,500 in 1958.

So what about his car? With millionaires such as sports figures and movie

stars driving expensive cars worth hundreds of thousands of dollars, you would expect a billionaire to drive something like a golden limo, right? Well, some do, but not Warren Buffett. This is one quiet billionaire that the same cheap car for years. The Cadillac XTS in question cost only $45,000 when he bought it in 2014, an upgrade from his former car a 2006 Cadillac DTS.

Some of the best financial advice you will ever find online are actually from Warren Buffett and the one advice of his applicable here is "**never plunge into the murky waters of investments without having some kind of a backup savings plan**".

Now, while there are a thousand ways to save money, the number of ways to save money and become rich are very few. Chief of them all is that you have to invest that savings and that is what Warren Buffett is indirectly talking about here. Before making any manner of investment with your money, be sure to put a small part of it away in a savings plan of some kind. This money will serve as a backup for the day disaster may hit.

Brian Williams

The best part of this investment/savings strategy, as I have found, is that it gives one more confidence and peace of mind in investments.

Brian Williams

2. Savings Are Not for The Poor Alone

The case of Warren Buffett, a billionaire who still saves greatly, should be an eye-opener for many. However, if you still believe that the art of saving money to become rich is only for the poor, sit down and calculate how much time you've been a working class person, then go and check how much your current account balance is.

Do the math and let the resulting tally speak for itself?

3. Get Paid Before Anyone Else

"**Pay Yourself First**" ... now, here is the number one rule of business and ironically enough, most people forget it in all their financial affairs in life.

Too many people spend their money before considering saving. This is actually a very dangerous path to walk. The situation should be the exact opposite, save before you spend. Pay yourself first before you pay anyone else.

Brian Williams

4. Stay Away from the Banks

Banks are the traditional institute for saving money the world over and here I am telling you to avoid them like the plague. This makes you think I am somewhat crazy, right? Not at all. According to some very successful saving experts, staying away from banks completely is one of the simplest ways to save money and become rich.

Let's dig further into the issue for facts and you will begin to see the reason why.

The Downside of Regular Banking

The banks only offer you the ability to do the following…

1. Conduct Transactions

The ability to conduct transactions with ease is the speculative function of money, keeping out the most important aspect of savings, which is precautionary.

Without even realizing it, all the transactions you conduct on your savings account makes the bank profits and you nothing. Basically, banks offer only the Speculative function of money, keeping out the most important aspect of savings, which, being purely precautionary, never leaves you with enough cash in your hands when you really need it on a rainy day.

2. The Fake Interest Rates

Unknown to so many people, banks only offer you a token sum of about 3.1% interest on whatever amount of money you save into the savings account you open with them. The catch is that you must never touch that money, but of course, they never make this very clear to customers. And this is part of the speculative function of money talked about above -- you assume that you are getting some interest on your savings while, in reality, you are not.

Without knowing it, we open a savings account and start making monthly deductions that all but cancels out every possible interest. We deposit a certain amount in the morning and before evening the next day, withdraw most of it again. Now ask yourself the smart question here, what is the essence of saving?

21

Brian Williams

3. The Bank's Love and Support

The greatest mistake business people and working-class people have always made is believing that their banks love them. The information in this book should help you get rid of that loser mentality. Ever wonder how the banks make all those tons of profit each year that makes all the rich businessmen want to own a bank?

The banks use customer savings for different kinds of investments of their own, from loan transactions to forex trading, all of which generate huge amounts of profits in very short periods of time. These kind of business ventures require huge amounts of capital and the bank gets that capital from the sum total of the countless numbers of accounts clients operate with them.

Now you know where the banks get the money to offer millions and billions in loans to needy businessmen and other organizations? They are also the biggest players in the forex market, which is the

Brian Williams

largest trading platform in the world with tens of trillions of dollars being moved around daily.

So you see, as long as you have a saving account, you never touch your bank loves you and at the end of each month they reward you with a few coins that will never make you rich even if multiplied tenfold. If you start making withdrawals from that account, the bank still loves you because they can now forget all about any interest they have to pay and get access to all your money for free, even if for one hour. Ten minutes, or better still, just one minute, is more than enough to make huge profits in the forex market, go ask any forex trading expert. You can never cheat a bank either way.

By putting your money in savings accounts, even if for a single day, you are actually helping the bank make huge profits but gain nothing in return. Between you and 50,000 other customers with savings accounts, you people actually provide the bank with a solid, interest-free, capital base over time. They make huge profits, you don't.

23

Brian Williams

Save Money Get Rich

Brian Williams

5. Consider Forced Longer-Term Investment Plans

Ben Simons, the low-level banker turned millionaire, who teaches people how to save money to grow rich, in one of his seminars, spoke of how he began his journey about a decade ago. He tried to help a friend as well at that time. They had a six-year plan in this case and the friend complained about the awful length of time required to save up his money and on the basis of this, declined the offer. According to Ben, this friend has worked for the seven years since with an account balance of less than $200,000, while he on his part, has quit his low-level bank job entirely, thanks to a net worth in the millions due to shrewd investment on the saved up money.

Simple research shows that American billionaire, Warren Buffett, walked this particular path several decades ago on the way to his immense wealth, but he wasn't the source of Ben's inspiration of the wealth planning strategy of saving to grow rich.

According to Ben, working in a financial institution gave him a lot of insight into the financial aspect of life. He has seen young people become millionaires merely by

25

wisely staving on a monthly basis for just a few years, while others who merely say they wanted to invest their money ended up doing nothing.

The key here, for young working-class people, is to consider investment plans of no less than 6 years to 9 years. This strategy also works for newlyweds (couples), and young mothers planning ahead for their children's education.

Investment Plan + Wise Saving =
Good Wealth Planning = Wealth

Now you know the secret and so the next level to go from here is where to get the tools to implement this secret.

Brian Williams

6. Where Then Do We Save Or Get These Special Plans?

The next smart question we want to be answered now is, where do we save our money or get such wonderful investment plans that guarantee we get rich after a while? Certainly not in the savings account of a bank. An insurance company is actually what you are looking for!

The type of investment plans we are talking about here actually have a form of protection embedded that cover the event where the breadwinner of the family dies. And here is just one reason why we recommend an Insurance Company for your savings.

Depending on your geographical location, there are different insurance firms offering different investment plans of this sort. We will look into this in an article that will be published for public accessibility here....

27

7. Have Just One Single Bank account and Multiple Investment accounts

One of the simplest ways to force yourself to accumulate wealth for your future and family is to have just one bank account but multiple investment accounts or plans. Bank accounts, which present the limitless possibility of withdrawals, expose you to the temptation of spending and spending more money, while investment plans, on the other hand, encourage you to save up for a goal or project.

A large number of wealthy people you see who buy up major assets such as real estate and entire companies almost on a yearly basis do not achieve all that with their bank accounts. They go for investment plans with insurance firms because, financial wizards that they are, they know exactly what is on offer.

I bet this is the first you are hearing about saving money with an investment firm or an insurance company!

Brian Williams

8. Draw Up Your Goals Clearly

Attaching a clear goal to your financial future will certainly go a long way in helping you make plans towards it. As a point say this, "if I save $10,000 monthly for 8 years, I will become a millionaire and invest in a good business".

Of course, all pockets are not the same size. What one person achieves in 8 years, another can achieve in just 2 years. The smaller your financial power, the longer it takes to save. Just plan right and then invest wisely. You could even become richer than the those who had bigger financial power than you did. And this is where an adequate backup plan comes in handy.

The art of financial investment is a risky business that can make you a lot of money in just one turn and then cost you all in another turn. Just go ask Warren Buffett, whose current company makes all kinds of investments that are supposed to be secure.

9. What is your Monthly Budget?

Getting through each month with a budget might be just what you need to ultimately make your dreams come true. Years ago, I used to earn just $5,000 monthly and I realized that to get out of financial difficulties for good, I had to force myself to start saving at least $2,500 monthly. It was by no means easy, but I achieved that feat through determination for 7 years. Even after I got a nice pay raise, I kept on with that particular savings scheme as a means of residual income. This money isn't much when imagined bit by bit, but just do the math. By the end of 7 years of saving, with no less than $30,000 and sometimes more going into my investment accounts each year, I had a substantial amount of money in my hands to go into big business.

Like Warren Buffett, I currently own several assets and amazing account balances, but my budget and overall spending have not changed. It is still quite minimal.

I am always on a budget and my wealth keeps growing.

The End

Brian Williams

Brian Williams

Author's Note

I don't do a lot of writing and my publishers handle all the work when it somes to publishing but try to read as the few books I have and you will understand why the rich get richer and the poor poorer in our society today.

Knowledge is power!

Brian Williams

FIND OTHER BOOKS BY THE AUTHOR

All book by the Author can be found on the publisher's websites listed below.

ABOUT THE PUBLISHER

Kingbooks is a brand under which a group of talented authors and intellectuals self-publish books in the different genres. We maintain a presence on the website of the founding author of the brand.

Visit Our Website Home page: Kingezesblog.com
Visit Our Web Page:
https://kingezesblog.com/kingbooks

Kingbooks: Entertainment and knowledge are our trade and we publish only the best books.

Brian Williams

NOTES

Brian Williams